ART ATTACK ™

Great Gifts

Hi! Welcome to
Art Attack!
This book is packed with terrific
ideas for gifts, so come inside
and get things all
wrapped up!

Mammoth

Contents

When you see this clock symbol, it means that you will have to leave your Art Attack to dry, often overnight.

WARNING
Be very careful when using sharp objects, such as scissors.

If you find it hard to cut through cardboard, try dampening it a little.

A safe way to make a hole in cardboard is to push the point of a hard pencil through the card into some sticky tack.

2

Perfect Papier Mâché

Many of the projects in this book need papier mâché. There are two ways of making this, but they both need the same glue mixture.
Pour some PVA glue into a bowl, then add half as much water. Stir them together to make a really strong mixture.

NEIL'S TIP
You can get PVA glue from any art supplies shop and most large stationery stores.

NEIL'S TIP
Make sure you protect your work surface with some old newspaper. If you work on a plastic bag you can simply peel off your project.

METHOD 1
This is ideal if you want to make a mould of something or if you want to cover something quite smoothly (e.g. Heavy-Weight Trainer, page 14).

Coat the item in the glue mixture, and cover it in strips of newspaper or toilet roll. You will probably need two or three layers.

Then paint over everything again with the glue mixture, and leave it to dry.

METHOD 2
This is perfect for modelling 3D shapes (e.g. 3D Badges, page 8).

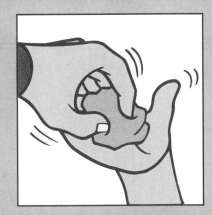

For this method, dip some newspaper or toilet roll into the glue mixture and squeeze out any excess glue. You can mould this into any shape you like and place it on your Art Attack. If you want, you can then cover everything in a layer of toilet roll to give a smoother outline, or just leave it to dry as it is.

Anything made with papier mâché will need time to dry out – at least overnight. So be patient.

Fantasy Flyer

Have you ever wondered how they design all those fantastic futuristic jets that you get in cartoons or computer games? They build a model first. Follow these steps to design a Fantasy Flyer for a fellow fanatic.

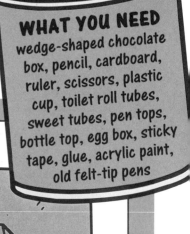

WHAT YOU NEED
wedge-shaped chocolate box, pencil, cardboard, ruler, scissors, plastic cup, toilet roll tubes, sweet tubes, pen tops, bottle top, egg box, sticky tape, glue, acrylic paint, old felt-tip pens

1

Lie the chocolate box on a piece of cardboard and draw a chunky pointed wing on each side. Take away the box and join up the wings.

2

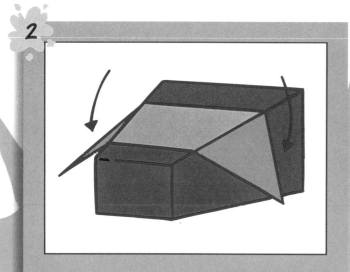

Cut the whole thing out and bend the wings slightly along the lines. Use a ruler to help you. Stick this on top of your chocolate box with the wings slanting down.

3

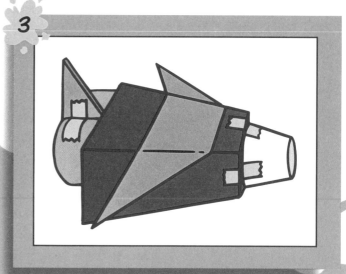

Tape a plastic cup to the front of the box for the nose. Cut a toilet roll tube in half and tape the sections to the back of the box for the jets. Cut out a triangle of cardboard and slot it between the tubes to make the tail. Stick it firmly in place.

4

To make your Fantasy Flyer look like a real aeroplane, stick on lots of tubes in all shapes and sizes. Some could go under the wings to look like jets and fuel tanks. Some could be cut in half to make interesting shapes.

5

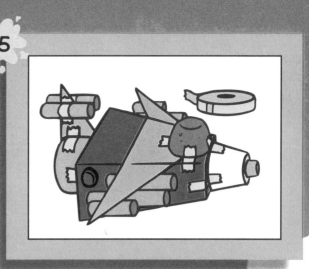

And to make it look really futuristic, stick on lots of other bits and pieces, for example a bottle-top nose, an egg box cockpit.

6

Make sure everything is stuck down firmly, then paint it – any colour you like. Add details in felt-tip or marker pen.

NEIL'S TIP
Instead of using acrylic paint, you can mix poster paint with PVA glue.

NEIL'S TIP
You might need to give your plane a few layers of paint, or start by giving it a white undercoat – especially if all your boxes and tubes are different colours.

Screaming Bookmark

Some people are always losing their place when they read a book. What they need is a bookmark – a screaming one!

WHAT YOU NEED
thin card, ruler, pencil, scissors, felt-tip pens, a book

1

Cut a strip of card roughly 6cm wide and twice the height of your book. Fold it in half, top to bottom. Then mark a point roughly a third of the way down from the fold and fold the top piece up again.

2

Draw the top lip of a mouth above the fold, and a bottom lip below the fold. Then draw the top and bottom half of a head, and make it look as gruesome as possible.

3

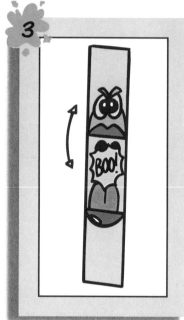

Open out your bookmark and draw an explosion box in the mouth. Write in it what you want to say. Then join up the two halves of the head behind the box. Add the details (tongue, teeth, tonsils) and colour everything in.

I know another way to make a bookmark scream – tell it a good ghost story! Ha ha ha!

4

Fold your bookmark back together and hook it over the page of your book. Then, when you pull your bookmark out from the top, it screams at you.

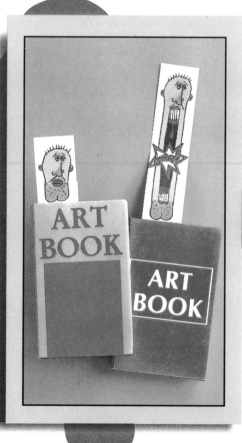

ART BOOK

ART BOOK

3D Books

If you want to give someone a really special present, without spending a fortune, try one of these 3D Books.

WHAT YOU NEED
blank book (hardback or paperback), papier mâché, pencil, paint, gold or silver pen, permanent marker

ALWAYS MAKE SURE YOU HAVE A WINDOW OPEN WHEN USING PERMANENT MARKERS!

NEIL'S TIP
It's a good idea to do the inside cover, too, as this stops the paper warping outwards as it dries.

1

Cover the front and back of your blank book in strips of papier mâché (see page 3) and leave to dry overnight.

2

Now draw your design on to your book. This one is going to be an ancient diary with fancy hinges, corner pieces and a lock.

3

When your design is finished, build it up by taking bits of tissue or newspaper and dipping them into the glue mixture. Squeeze out the excess, then press into shape on the cover.
Leave to dry overnight again.

4

When the book is dry, you can paint it.

5

Add the metal details in gold or silver pen. Use a permanent marker to add outline or shadows.

Brilliant 3D Badges

Badges are great and they make really fun presents, especially these fantastic 3D Art Attack badges!

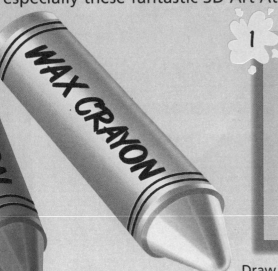

WHAT YOU NEED
cardboard, pencil, scissors, larg safety pin, sticky tape, PVA glue toilet paper, papier mâché, paint black marker pen, plastic bag to work on

1. Draw your badge shape on to a piece of cardboard. Cut it out and tape a safety pin to the back, as near the middle as possible.

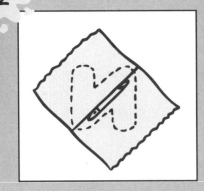

2. Brush some PVA glue over the back of your badge. Place a piece of toilet paper on top, butting up to the pin. Then place another piece on the other side of the pin. Leave to dry, then trim off the edges.

3. Now for the front of your badge! Mould a 3D shape out of papier mâché, then leave it to dry and harden overnight.

4. When it's completely dry, paint on your design and draw round the edge with a black marker pen.

NEIL'S TIP
Make sure you stick down the fixed side of the pin, not the side that opens. Otherwise, you won't be able to wear your badge!

Try any design you like!

Giant Pencil

Do you know someone who never has a pen or pencil? Well, give them one of these giant Art Attack pencils and they'll never be stuck for something to write with.

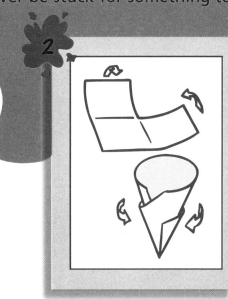

WHAT YOU NEED
front and back of a cereal box, pencil, ruler, sticky tape, scissors, felt-tip pen, newspaper, papier mâché, paint, gold or silver pen

1 Divide one of the cereal box sides widthways into six equal strips. Fold the card along these lines. Overlap and tape the two end strips. This is the body of the pencil.

2 Cut out a quarter of the other piece of cereal box and roll it into a cone. Place it in one end of the pencil and let it spring out to fit snugly. Tape it in place.

3 Snip enough off the end to fit your felt-tip pen. Slip the pen inside (with the lid on) and tape that in place too, with at least half a centimetre poking out above the lid.

4 Now stuff the pencil tightly with scrunched-up newspaper. When it is packed, tape across the top to keep everything in. Cover all except the tip in papier mâché and leave to dry overnight.

5 When it's dry you can paint it and add lettering in gold or silver – just like a real pencil.

It even writes, and if it ever runs out, just pull out the pen and replace it with another.

Wind-Up Tongue Card

This is the perfect way to wind up your family and friends.

1

Fold a piece of card in half. Draw a line on the inside about 9cm long (that's a bit longer than your finger). This is the mouth. Draw or paint a funny face around it – the uglier the better!

2

Make a hole at each end of the line, 1cm below it. Make another hole in the middle of the line. Put your scissors through and snip along the line – but don't go quite as far as the other two holes.

WHAT YOU NEED
card, pencil, paint or felt-tip pens, sticky tack, scissors, elastic band, paper clips, sticky tape

3

From the back of the card, poke the ends of an elastic band through the two holes and slip them on to the paper clip.

4

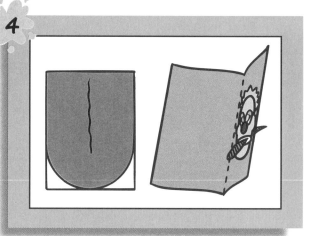

On another piece of card, draw a rectangle 8cm by 11cm with a tongue shape at the bottom. Cut it out and colour it in. Slot the tongue into the mouth and tape it at the back.

5

Now your card's ready. Twist the elastic band with the paper clip. When it's fully wound up, trap it with the tongue, close the card and keep it shut with another paper clip.

Now you just have to decide who you want to wind up today. Stand back and wait for the raspberry!

10

Gift Wrapping Paper

This Art Attack could save you a lot of pocket money. Try making your own wrapping paper.

WHAT YOU NEED
a large sheet of paper, felt-tip pens, gold or silver pen

1

With a felt-tip pen, draw a cross down the middle of your sheet of paper. I like red felt tip on white paper.

2

In the two top sections, draw loops that join in the middle. In the two bottom sections, draw long thin triangles that also join in the middle. Then colour the whole thing in.

3

Decorate all the red that you've drawn with your gold or silver pen. Then carefully draw a circle in the middle. This is your bow.

4

Add shadows to your bow to make it stand out from the paper. Do this by drawing a dark line on all the bottom and left-hand edges.

Now draw and decorate a rectangle in the bottom right-hand section of the paper and write your message inside. Draw a little circle and some string to the middle, and there you have some DIY wrapping paper, complete with its own gift tag.

Well, that just about wraps it up!

Stained-Glass Picture

Why not liven up someone's view with this Stained-Glass Picture?

WHAT YOU NEED
paper, pencil, tissue paper, PVA glue, sticky-backed plastic, cardboard, scissors

Draw a simple design for your picture. Then tear pieces of tissue paper roughly into the shapes that you have drawn.

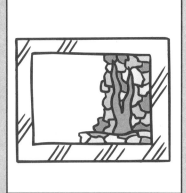

Pour a cup of PVA glue on to a sheet of sticky-backed plastic (shiny side up). Paste it into a rectangle the same size as your design. Stick the tissue paper shapes down. Fill in the gaps with small scraps of tissue paper for a mosaic effect.

Carefully pour more PVA glue on top and spread it out without moving the shapes. Leave it to dry – for about 3 days!

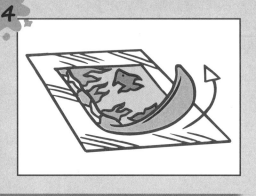

Now just hold your picture up to the light to get a great stained-glass effect.

When your picture is dry, peel it away from the sticky-backed plastic and turn it over, so that the underneath side is facing upwards. Cut out a cardboard frame and stick it on.

Slot Plants

Are you ever stuck for an idea for a present? Well, everyone loves a plant, and you don't even have to water these!

WHAT YOU NEED
cardboard box, scissors, pencil, ruler, paint, marker pen

1

Cut two sides off a cardboard box and draw a vertical line down the middle of each one.

2

Now draw a flower or plant using this line as centre. Do a simple, big, bold shape, and make sure that the bottom is absolutely straight. Cut out your shape and draw around it on the second piece of card, making sure that the two centre lines line up. Cut this out, too.

NEIL'S TIP
To make sure that the slot is the right thickness, stand a straight piece of card up on its edge along the line, and draw round it.

3

Using the centre lines, measure halfway up both cut-outs and mark a point. Draw from this point up to the top of one shape and down to the bottom of the other shape. Now cut a slot the exact thickness of the cardboard along the lines you have drawn.

4

Paint both sides of your plant. Don't forget the pot.

Blooming marvellous!

When they're dry, add details in permanent marker. Then just slot the two pieces together and stand them up.

Heavy-Weight Trainer

Next time you are about to throw out an old pair of worn trainers or shoes – don't! Turn them into fantastic heavy-weight doorstops, bookends or paperweights.

WHAT YOU NEED
an old shoe, small stones, paper cup, scissors, sticky tape, papier mâché, felt-tip pen, paint

1

Take an old shoe. Remove the laces, and fasten any buckles or straps. Pack the shoe with stones, right into all the nooks and crannies.

2

Place a paper cup inside the shoe, where your heel would normally go. You may have to take out a few stones. Cut or tear the cup so that it's level with the mouth of the shoe. Tape it firmly in place.

3

Cover the whole thing, even inside the cup, with two layers of papier mâché. Then leave it to dry overnight.

Draw on your design and paint your shoe in bright, bold colours.

NEIL'S TIP
If your shoe is a bit smelly, wash it first and let it dry.

Here's a footnote: These are definitely not running shoes!

Creepy Mobiles

If you want to give someone a terrifying scrap attack, these creepy mobiles are just perfect!

WHAT YOU NEED
scrap paper –
black, white and red, PVA glue,
felt-tip pen, cotton thread,
sticky tape

1

Scrunch up a piece of black scrap paper into a ball in the palm of your hand – this is the creature's 'body'.

2

Take a piece of black paper about 10cm square and twist to make it long and thin. Do the same with another five pieces of paper – these are the creature's 'legs'.

3

Dip one of the 'legs' in the PVA glue and stick it into a crack in the 'body'. Bend it down a little. Do the same for the other five 'legs', sticking three on each side of the 'body'.

4

Scrunch up two small pieces of white paper into very tight balls – these are the 'eyes'. With a felt-tip pen, draw on the 'eyeballs'. Cut a small piece of red paper into a rough oval shape – this is the 'tongue'. Dip the 'eyes' and 'tongue' in the PVA glue and stick them in place on the 'body'.

5

Brush PVA glue all over the creature, including the 'eyes' and 'tongue' and leave to dry overnight until it is hard and shiny.

Stick a length of cotton thread on to the creature's back with sticky tape, hang it up and wait for the screams!

To make other mobiles, you could add glitter eyes and scrap paper teeth, or tracing paper wings and a long curly tongue made by twisting a piece of paper round a pencil. Or make up your own creepy creatures!

Thumbs-Up Award

Say 'well done' to someone who has passed a test or achieved something really great with a Thumbs-Up Award.

WHAT YOU NEED
cardboard, pencil, scissors, newspaper, sticky tape, polystyrene cup, pebble, papier mâché, paint

Draw round your hand on to a piece of card. Include about 5cm of your wrist. Make sure your fingers are together and the thumb is sticking out to one side. Cut it out, snipping between the fingers.

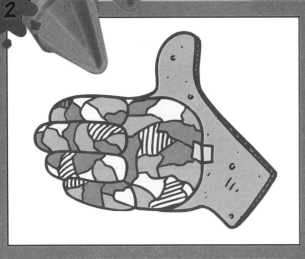

Scrunch up a sheet of newspaper and tape it to one side of the hand. Twist smaller bits of newspaper and tape them to each finger. This is now the back of your hand. Tape more newspaper twists to the fingers on the other side.

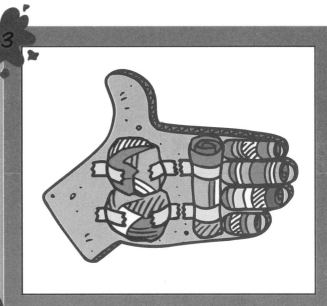

Scrunch half a page of newspaper into a sausage and tape it below the fingers. Tape two small balls of newspaper just above the wrist in the same place as the bumps on your own hand. Wrap more sticky tape round the fingers and palm to make it sturdier.

4

Now bend the fingers (not the thumb) one by one, and hold them closed. Tape them into position.

5

Tape the polystyrene cup upside down in the middle of a square of cardboard. Tear off the top, then cut about a quarter of the way down each side. Put a pebble in the cup to act as a weight and stuff a ball of newspaper on top of it to keep it in place.

6

Push the wrist of the hand into the slot in the cup, and tape it firmly in place.

7

Cover the whole thing, including the base, in two layers of papier mâché, moulding some more knuckles and bumps if you want. Leave it to dry.

When dry, paint the base black and the hand gold or silver. You can add some shading in the nooks and crannies, too.

NEIL'S TIP

Make your own gold-effect paint by adding a tiny bit of black and green to your yellow paint.

WAX CRAYON

A Celebration Breakfast

Why not make a celebration breakfast for someone special? An Art Attack Celebration Breakfast, that is.

WHAT YOU NEED
white card, pencil, cotton wool, tissue paper (various colours), PVA glue, felt-tip pens, scissors, backing paper or board

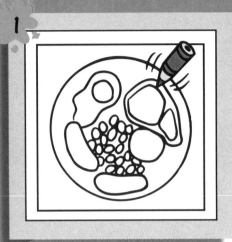

Draw a dinner plate sized circle on your white card. On this plate roughly draw an egg, sausages, beans, a chop and a tomato.

Dab some PVA glue mixed with a touch of water on to just one area of the picture. Stick on some cotton w

Cover the cotton wool with coloured tissue paper and paste down the edges, stuffing the cotton wool in as you go.

Build up the whole picture in this way, section by section.

When the glue is dry, add some more detail with a felt-tip pen, or scraps of tissue paper.

Mmmm! Looks nice enough to eat!

When you've finished, cut the whole thing out. If you like, you can stick it on to some coloured paper or board

Dream Island

Do you know anyone who loves going on holiday?
Now you can make them their own paradise island in the sun.

WHAT YOU NEED
cardboard (at least A4 size), pencil, newspaper, PVA glue, papier mâché, small card squares, paint, clingfilm

1

Start by drawing a rough outline of your island on the cardboard. Leave enough space around the edge for the sea.

2

You then create the shape of your island using scrunched-up balls of newspaper. Dip the bottom of each ball into some PVA glue mixed with water. Then stick it in place.

3

When you are happy with the overall shape of your island, cover it all in strips of papier mâché. Push it into the newspaper to make coves and interesting rock formations. Leave to dry overnight.

4

Add some trees, made from small balls of newspaper covered in PVA mixture. Also add some buildings – small square scraps of card and a folded piece of card for the roofs. Leave to dry again.

5

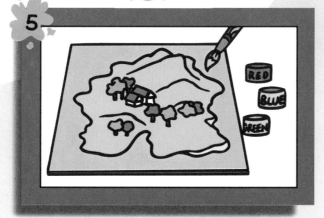

Now paint your island. To create shimmering surf, stick bits of clingfilm on to the sea and wrinkle it up to form waves.

6

And here's a very special paradise island.

Heart-Throb Brooch

Do you know anyone with a secret heart-throb?
Try making this Heart-Throb Brooch for them.

WHAT YOU NEED
an empty matchbox,
paper, pencil,
scissors, safety pin,
sticky tape, glue,
card, glitter, picture

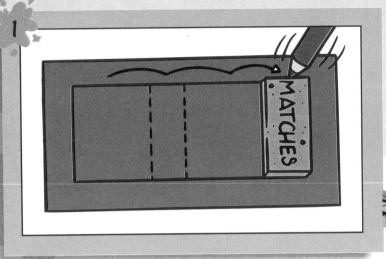

NEIL'S TIP
If you do this on coloured paper or wrapping paper, you won't need to paint it later.

Place the matchbox on your paper and draw around three sides. Roll the matchbox along the paper, drawing along the edges as you go. Cut out this long strip of paper, and it should fit perfectly round the matchbox.

Now make the shape for the front of your brooch. Cut it out, cover it with glue and dip it in some glitter. When it's dry, stick it to the front of the box.

Tape a safety pin to the back of the box. Make sure you tape the side of the pin that doesn't open. Cover one side of the paper in glue and wrap it round the box, starting at the pin.

Stick your heart-throb picture on the inside of the matchbox. Then you can slip the inside back into the box and no one will know that the picture is there.

I liked mine so much I kept it myself.

Comic Strip Photo Frames

WHAT YOU NEED
A3 paper, felt-tip pens, pencil, scissors, glue, photos

Do you want to see someone star in a comic strip? Well, here's your chance.

1

Fold your piece of paper in half lengthways. Then fold it in half the other way. Fold the top flap down in half, then turn over the paper and do the same to the other flap.

NEIL'S TIP
Don't worry if the lines are wobbly. It all adds to the effect.

2

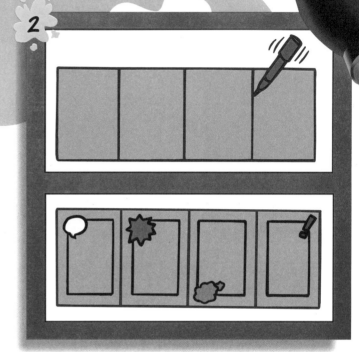

Lay your strip flat with the folded side to the bottom. Draw a felt-tip line along the top of the paper, as close to the edge as possible. Draw lines down each crease, too. Draw a pencil frame about 2cm wide in each of the boxes and add some comic strip special effects, such as speech and thought bubbles, or explosion boxes. Go over these neatly in felt-tip.

3

Open out the paper. To cut out the windows, make a hole the safe way (see page 2) and use this as a starting point for your scissors. Dab some glue carefully down each crease and down the side edges. Leave the top open. Fold the paper back over and press it down. Leave it overnight with some books on top.

4

When the glue is dry, trim some photos to fit the frames and slide them in. Write some messages in the special effects boxes and you've got your own personal comic strip.

Surprise Birthday Cards

These pictures look quite normal, but open the flap and you get a big surprise. These surprise pictures make ideal birthday cards for your friends.

1

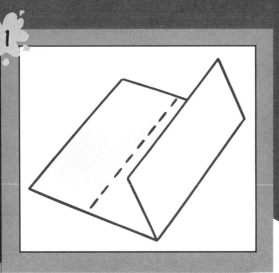

Take a piece of thin card (any size you like) and divide it into thirds along the top. Fold over the right-hand third.

2

Think of an idea for your card and draw it across the front on both pieces. Make sure that anything that you want to change on the inside goes on the right hand flap.

Snappy birthday!

3

fold

fold

Open out the flap so that you only have half a picture. Now you can change whatever you like on the right-hand side of the picture. First draw in all the bits that you don't want to change. Then draw in your surprise and colour it in.

ART ATTACK

22

Design a T-Shirt

No ideas for your best friend's birthday present? Why not create a fantastic exclusive T-shirt with this simple method?

NEIL'S TIP

If you draw your design on to your T-shirt in pencil, you can rub it out if you make a mistake.

WHAT YOU NEED
a plain T-shirt, cardboard, pencil, permanent markers, gold pen

Put a piece of cardboard inside a plain white T-shirt. This helps to stretch the area you want to draw on. It also stops the ink going through to the back of your T-shirt.

Now draw your design on to the T-shirt using lightly flicked lines.

Take care when washing your new fancy T-shirt. Make sure the water isn't too hot. You may find that the colour fades over time, but then you can just go over the design with your pens again.

When you've finished your outline, fill it in with coloured permanent marker. Add special jazzy gold pen for a bit of extra dazzle.

Art Chart

Name	Great Gift